LOSS OF A DREAM

IN THIS

Devotions for

VERY

Your Time of Need

HOUR

LOSS OF A DREAM

IN THIS

Devotions for

VERY

Your Time of Need

HOUR

ROBIN PRINCE MONROE

BROADMAN
& HOLMAN
PUBLISHERS

Nashville, Tennessee

Printed in the United States of America

4253-77
0-8054-5377-6

Dewey Decimal Classification: 242.4
Subject Heading:
DEVOTIONAL LITERATURE
Library of Congress Card Catalog Number: 94-5002

Unless otherwise indicated, all Scripture references are from
the Holy Bible,
New International Version, copyright © 1973, 1978, 1984
by International Bible Society.

Library of Congress Cataloging-in-Publication Data
Monroe, Robin Prince, 1956–
   Devotions for your time of need.
Loss of a dream / by Robin Prince Monroe.
   p.   cm. — (In this very hour)
   ISBN 0-8054-5377-6
   1. Consolation.   2. Loss (Psychology)—Religious aspects—
Christianity—Prayer-books and devotions—English.
I. Title.   II. Series.
BV4909.M65   1994
242'.4—dc20   94-5002
                                                                            CIP

To Caleb, Anna, Daniel, and Lydia—
my dreams come true.

All my longings lie open before you,
O Lord; my sighing is not hidden from you.
Psalm 38:9

Contents

PROLOGUE

WHEN DREAMS DIE

I remember being full of dreams. What happened? Now I often find myself dragging through the day with an empty loneliness, with a sense of "Is this it? Is this all there is?"

It was a long time before I understood the source of my malaise. Finally, through the Spirit's constant, gentle nudges, I realized that I was grieving. I was grieving over the loss of some of my dreams, and just like grief over a death, I was experiencing denial, anger, and pain.

When you were younger, how did you picture your future? Chances are that your life is different from what you pictured. Life brings unexpected changes, some that you have probably welcomed. But sometimes when you realize that a dream will never come true, there is a terrible sense of loss.

The dream may seem insignificant, such as realizing you will never make that trip to Alaska. Or it may be life shattering, like an injury that means you will never play pro ball. But your dreams are important no matter how small or large.

Our dreams are a part of who we are, a part of who God made us to be. When we lose a dream, we lose a part of ourselves.

While in college, I dreamed of teaching deaf children. I put all my young energy into learning sign language so I would someday be able to teach the hearing impaired. I also dreamed of being a writer. I had taken a course in children's literature and was enchanted by the more than fifty books we were required to read. In my heart somewhere I tucked away the dream of writing a children's book. These were my conscious dreams.

During that time I had unspoken dreams. I longed to find the right man to be my husband. I thought about having children and what it might be like to be a mom. I longed for a family of my own, and I pictured that family in my heart. These were the dreams I kept quietly hidden in some secret place.

When I was in my second year of college, I met Merlin. I fell in love completely but reluctantly, in an attempt to guard my heart. We were married the summer after graduation. Now, all my dreams for the future were intertwined with the dreams of this other dear person.

In our second year of marriage we moved to Greenville, South Carolina, where John Caleb was born and a year and a half later his sister Anna Elizabeth. The longing for a family of my own was being answered.

I decided to stay at home with the kids, and Merlin worked extra hard to make that possible. I had been around children all my life, but there was no way I could be ready for the reality of taking care of my own children. Even all my experience couldn't prepare me for the sudden knowledge that everything I said or did made a difference in how well this little person might do in life. Being a good mom was the hardest thing I had ever tried to do, and soon my whole being was wrapped up in it.

We enjoyed our children immensely, and after Merlin found a good job, we decided the time was right to have another baby. Caleb was six and Anna was four and a half when Daniel Aaron was born.

When he was four months old, Daniel was hospitalized because of respiratory difficulties. Though he didn't have some of the physical characteristics, the doctor suspected that he had Down's syndrome. He was tested at that time, and the doctor's suspicions were confirmed.

All parents have dreams for their children—dreams for their future, what careers they might choose, and how many children they might have. Then there are all the little dreams—the first time they tie their shoes or read a book or learn to swim or play in a recital. And then there are the even smaller dreams—the first time they take a step or eat by themselves or learn to "go potty" or say their first word.

It soon became apparent that for Daniel most of the "big" dreams just wouldn't come true. Because of seizures and chronic illness even many of the smaller dreams would not either. So we kept working toward the tiny dreams. My prayer for Daniel became simple: "Please, Lord, keep our little boy well, and help him to learn to walk and feed himself and to take care of his bathroom needs." These things we took for granted with our other children, but they were huge dreams for Daniel.

When Daniel was two, our precious Anna died suddenly of unsuspected leukemia. Our hearts were broken. I remember sitting at the hospital with Merlin and saying to him, "But I was going to help her take care of her babies. She's only a little girl. She'll never know the joy of being a mama. . . ."

Or the sorrow. So many of my dreams died with her.

℃

1

GOD KNOWS OUR LONGINGS

All my longings lie open before you, O Lord;
my sighing is not hidden from you.

Psalm 38:9

Sometimes we think we know exactly what we want, but our knowledge is limited by how well we know ourselves. Only God knows us completely, and our longings are not hidden from Him.

2

IT'S OKAY TO BE OVERWHELMED

They went to a place called Gethsemane, and Jesus said to his disciples, "Sit here while I pray." He took Peter, James and John along with him, and he began to be deeply distressed and troubled. "My soul is overwhelmed with sorrow to the point of death," he said to them. "Stay here and keep watch."

Going a little farther, he fell to the ground and prayed that if possible the hour might pass from him. "Abba, Father," he said, "everything is possible for you. Take this cup from me. Yet not what I will, but what you will."

Mark 14:32–36

Jesus, the perfect Son of God, was overwhelmed with what he saw he was about to face. He knew He would be required to die a painful death, and He knew His Father could change His circumstances in a moment. He prayed for a change.

It's okay to want your circumstances to change, and it is not sinful to be overwhelmed.

3

WE DON'T ALWAYS KNOW WHAT WE NEED

In the same way, the Spirit helps us in our weakness. We do not know what we ought to pray, but the Spirit himself intercedes for us with groans that words cannot express. And he who searches our hearts knows the mind of the Spirit, because the Spirit intercedes for the saints in accordance with God's will.

Romans 8:26–27

In *The Tapestry,* Edith Shaeffer compares our lives to a huge tapestry. We can only see the back, and often all we see are a number of dark threads. It doesn't look like we think it should. It's tangled and the colors are all muddled. But God sees the front, and He weaves the threads, light and dark together to form the beautiful, purposeful picture of our lives.

Our vision is very limited, and we really don't know what we need. In some mysterious way, God uses even the losses in our lives to make the picture more beautiful.

Our son Daniel has an immune problem so he is not able to go to school. The school system sends a teacher to our home. Staying home to care for Daniel ties me down and that has been hard for me because I love to be involved. I can't volunteer very often at Caleb's and Lydia's schools. I don't make it to the women's Bible study or the concerned parents' prayer group. But God has used this very thing to keep me still long enough to write. He took away something I desired and replaced it with a new dream, and perhaps, a better one.

4

LIFE IS FRUSTRATING

For the creation was subjected to frustration, not by its own choice, but by the will of the one who subjected it, in hope that the creation itself will be liberated from its bondage to decay and brought into the glorious freedom of the children of God.

Romans 8:20–21

"The creation was subjected to frustration." Sometimes I feel like a fly at a window. I see the light and dream about reaching it; then I buzz full speed ahead trying to get out. Instead I crash again and again into the glass. The light is beautiful, and there is nothing wrong with trying to reach it; but only God can open the window and often, for our own good, He chooses not to. Then when God does open the window, we're often either too discouraged, too afraid, or even too lazy to fly out. I know God has had to brush me off the sill more than once.

Maybe for you the light represents a godly mate, a steady job, a slimmer figure, or a home of your own. God doesn't promise that in this lifetime all your desires will be met. He tells us we will be frustrated with this world, but He also promises that even in the midst of our frustrations we can find joy.

5

GOD'S WAYS ARE HIGHER

"For my thoughts are not your thoughts, neither are your ways my ways," declares the Lord. "As the heavens are higher than the earth, so are my ways higher than your ways."

Isaiah 55:8–9

When I read this verse I picture God walking in front of me along a trail. We come to a fork. One path leads upward; it is steep and rocky and overgrown with briars. The other path leads to the right. I can tell that it would be a beautiful way to go—it appears smooth and clear and is obviously a much easier route to take.

God says, "This is where I want you to go."

I plead with God, "Please, please let me go down the easier path."

But God firmly says, "No, you need to go this way. Don't worry, I'll be right beside you. I'll hold your hand, and if you find you can't go on, I'll carry you."

There were almost two months between the time that Daniel was tested for Down's syndrome and when we received the results. During those two months I pleaded with God. I begged Him to let those tests come back negative, to let me take the other trail. When the doctor called us and told us that our baby had Down's, all I could see was the steep, rocky climb before me. At first all I noticed was how tired I was and how much I hurt. But after a time, I started to glance up occasionally and I could see things I had never seen before.

I pictured God smiling at me and saying, "Do you understand now? You would have never seen all this if I had let you take the other path."

God's plans are different—and higher—from ours.

6

WHY IS THERE PAIN?

And I heard a loud voice from the throne saying, "Now the dwelling of God is with men, and he will live with them. They will be his people, and

God himself will be with them and be their God. He will wipe every tear from their eyes. There will be no more death or mourning or crying or pain, for the old order of things has passed away."

Revelation 21:3–4

For God so loved the world that he gave his one and only Son, that whoever believes in him shall not perish but have eternal life. For God did not send his Son into the world to condemn the world, but to save the world through him.

John 3:16–17

God is the ultimate recycler. In nature, everything that dies somehow contributes to new life. Leaves fall from the trees, rot, and become compost which replenishes the soil. Animals kill other ainmals for food. Even feces is used as a breeding place for insects or a fertilizer for plants. God wastes nothing. Neither does God waste anything that happens in our lives. He takes our most painful experiences, even the messes we make ourselves, and brings good out of them.

Why is there pain in the world? I don't believe there is a clear or simple answer to this question, but here is an attempt to explain what I understand:

Although our own pain is not always the result of our personal sin, sin, in a larger sense, is the reason pain and disease entered Eden. Sin entered the world and altered it so completely that struggle became a part of man's everyday existence (see Gen. 3).

From Genesis 3 on, the Bible's central message is redemption. It is about how God chose not to wipe us out. It is the story of how a holy God who cannot tolerate sin made a way for us to be sinless.

Had God chosen simply to remove all the pain, He would have had to remove all the sin and therefore obliterate all the sinners. He loves us too much to give us a painless world. Instead, for now, He allows sin and pain to exist to give us time to receive the sinless nature of His Son.

He promises us that if we receive the forgiveness He has provided through Christ we will someday know a sinless, painless world. That promise gives us hope as we muddle through the hurt of our lost dreams. And like fruit trees greener and heavier with fruit because they are planted in manure, God makes us flourish even in an odious world.

7

It's Okay to Mourn

In the land of Uz there lived a man whose name was Job. This man was blameless and upright; he feared God and shunned evil. . . .

"Your sons and daughters were feasting and drinking wine at the eldest brother's house, when suddenly a mighty wind swept in from the desert and struck the four corners of the house. It collapsed on them and they are dead, and I am the only one who has escaped to tell you!"

At this, Job got up and tore his robe and shaved his head. Then he fell to the ground in worship and said: "Naked I came from my mother's womb, and naked I will depart. The Lord gave and the Lord has taken away; may the name of the Lord be praised."

Job 1:1, 18–21

There are different ways to lose our dreams. Sometimes you realize that you will not be able to obtain something that you had longed for. Sometimes you obtain a dream, only to have it crumble before your eyes.

Job had a dream life. He was a respected man of God. He had a fine family. He was even wealthy. Then, in just a few hours everything was gone.

Job went into mourning. He tore at his robe and shaved his head. But even as he lay in desperate pain he recognized that God was in control.

8

We Need Room to Grieve

In all this, Job did not sin by charging God with wrongdoing.

Job 1:22

Yet when I hoped for good, evil came; when I looked for light, then came darkness. The churning inside me never stops; days of suffering confront me.

Job 30:26–27

When Job's grief was new he was able to praise God. As time passed and his great heartache and pain continued, it became increasingly difficult for him to praise. He began to question God. Two things are apparent to me as I read his heart-rendering prayers.

First, Job was very honest with God. He simply blurted out everything he felt. He knew God before his tragedies, and I think he understood that God already knew his feelings anyway.

Second, in spite of what appeared to be a long silence from God, Job continued to go to God with all his questions and complaints. Even through the pain, questioning, and turmoil, Job continued his relationship with God. God patiently listened to Job for a long time before He spoke. He gave Job room to grieve. We would do well if we could learn to give ourselves and others that same space.

9

God's Incredible Mercy

Then Job said to the Lord: "I know that you can do all things; no plan of yours can be thwarted.

[You asked,] Who is this that obscures my counsel without knowledge?" Surely I spoke of things
I did not understand, things too wonderful for
me to know."

Job 42:1–3

If you have some time today read Job chapters 38–41.

After a time of silence, God spoke to Job. Since I've
become a Christian I've heard teaching about this
book several times. Each time the focus was on Job's
sin of daring to question the God of the universe. But
God didn't end this book in rebuke. He ended it with
restoration and mercy. When we really remember
who God is, then it becomes apparent how great His
love for us must be. The fact that the Almighty God
cares about our personal situations is incredible!

10

REAL JOY

Now is your time of grief, but I will see you again
and you will rejoice, and no one will take away
your joy.

John 16:22

May the God of hope fill you with all joy and
peace as you trust in him, so that you may overflow with hope by the power of the Holy Spirit.

Romans 15:13

A dictionary defines joy as "a condition or feeling of high pleasure or delight, happiness, gladness." The Bible, however, defines joy as something much more significant. It is a quality of God that characterizes the life of one who believes in Him and that will characterize the life a believer will have with Him in heaven.

In the midst of my grief and disappointment I would sometimes ask myself, "Where is the joy?" From my perspective in the middle of the pain I couldn't see God working.

But God enabled me to struggle through those times, and each small step was a confirmation of my trust in Him. The joy I began to experience was very different from the kind of joy I had known before, but it was joy.

Instead of an emotional upwelling, it was a small assurance. It wasn't something I could point to and say, "See, over there, I still have joy." In fact, I'm very sure no one around me—except God—could even sense there was any joy at all. It was the littlest spark that kept my heart from going cold.

Christ said, "Now is your time of grief, but I will see you again and you will rejoice, and no one will take away your joy." In that one sentence He gave us permission to hurt, and then He set before us the promise of a joy that lasts forever. A joy which is rooted in Him but floriated with tremendous emotional upwelling.

11

MOSES LOST A DREAM

"Therefore, you will see the land only from a
distance; you will not enter the land I am giving
to the people of Israel."

Deuteronomy 32:52

Moses spent the better part of his life working toward
his dream—to enter the promised land with his people. He faced doubts about his ability to lead. He
confronted the King of Egypt. He encountered the
obstacle of the Red Sea. He led a whining, unfaithful
people for forty years through a desert. Then, when
he was almost there, God said, "Go climb that moun-
tain, and look at the land, but you will die before you
enter" (paraphrased). Moses' dream would come to
pass for his people, but never for himself.

Deuteronomy 32:51 tells us Moses wasn't allowed
to enter Canaan because of his sin. God was disciplin-
ing him. Losing a dream may be the result of sin.
Often however, that isn't the case. Job was blameless
and upright (Job 1:1) when tragedy hit his life.

It breaks my heart to think that after all those years
Moses wasn't allowed to achieve his dream, but I am
greatly encouraged as I look at Moses' special relationship with God. God dealt with the sin in Moses'
life—and that was painful—but Moses knew God
face to face (Deut. 34:10). Imagine! Face to face!

12

THE ULTIMATE DREAM

I know that my Redeemer lives, and that in the end he will stand upon the earth. And after my skin has been destroyed, yet in my flesh I will see God; I myself will see him with my own eyes—I, and not another. How my heart yearns within me!

Job 19:25–27

No matter how disappointed we become, no matter how many of our dreams are shattered, God has given us a dream that will never die—the dream of heaven. Someday we will stand in God's presence and all the pain that sin has brought into our lives will be gone forever.

There are days that you don't have the energy or hope to even try to rebuild your earthly dreams. On those days, fix your mind and heart on the ultimate dream—heaven.

13

GOD CARES

Why do you say, O Jacob, and complain, O Israel, "My way is hidden from the Lord; my cause is disregarded by my God"? Do you not know? Have you not heard? The Lord is the everlasting God, the Creator of the ends of the earth. He will not grow tired or weary, and his understanding no one can fathom.

Isaiah 40:27–28

When you are hurting and God doesn't seem anywhere to be found, it is easy to say to yourself, "God must not care." You might even feel in your heart that He is just too busy with other things. It's only natural to have those feelings because often this is our experience in human relationships.

But God isn't like our sinful human companions. He is the everlasting God, the Creator. He never gets too tired for us or too busy, and He understands our "causes" much better than we do ourselves.

14

A FUTURE AND A HOPE

"For I know the plans I have for you," declares the Lord, "plans to prosper you and not to harm you, plans to give you hope and a future. Then you will call upon me and come and pray to me, and I will listen to you. You will seek me and find me when you seek me with all your heart."

Jeremiah 29:11–13

Our son Daniel is profoundly retarded. That means that when the school psychologist tests him, his scores are in the very lowest range. He is eight years old and can't feed himself or walk or talk. He is like a baby, only bigger.

Sometimes I look at this precious son and I feel hopeful. He says "MaMa," and he stands alone. Maybe he will learn enough so I can continue to care for him at home.

Other days it's hard to keep trying. He has been standing alone for three years, and we still haven't been able to coax him to take his first step. He has been saying "MaMa" for two years now, and though sometimes he makes other sounds that can seem like words, he really has yet to use any other sounds with meaning.

I can picture the future for my other children. I can see them going off to college and then having families of their own. But I can't begin to imagine Daniel's future. I can't come up with a plan that I feel I can live with.

But despite my limited vision, God *already* has a plan in place for Daniel—a plan to prosper him and not to harm him; a plan to give our family a future and a hope.

I don't know what dream you have lost. But I know very well that when some dreams are destroyed it becomes difficult to imagine a hopeful future. But God has promised us a future and a hope. We have to cling to that promise even when we can't see past today.

15

STRENGTH RENEWED

Even youths grow tired and weary, and young men stumble and fall; but those who hope in the Lord will renew their strength. They will soar on wings like eagles; they will run and not grow weary, they will walk and not be faint.

Isaiah 40:30–31

After you grieve over the loss of your dream and then learn to accept your loss, the time to start dreaming will come again.

You will be tired. You may be so tired that you can't think straight. There is a beautiful promise in these verses: "those who hope in the Lord will renew their strength." Place your hope for the future in God. Not only will He give you the strength to carry on; He will enable you to soar like an eagle!

16

SEEK GOD'S COUNSEL

But Jehoshaphat also said to the king of Israel, "First seek the counsel of the Lord."

1 Kings 22:5

You have moved past your hurt, and you have the strength to dream again. Now what?

Begin to look at the world as a place full of possibilities. First, ask yourself the question: If I could do anything I wanted to do, what would it be?

Next, write *every* possibility down. One by one, bring your ideas before the Lord. Don't *you* let your present circumstances or past failures close any of the doors that God may be desiring to open for you.

God can overcome any circumstance. No matter how incredible each idea seems, present it to God. Pray with hope in your heart and with the willingness to relinquish each dream to Him.

17

SEEK OTHER'S ADVICE

Plans fail for lack of counsel, but with many advisers they succeed. A man finds joy in giving an apt reply—and how good is a timely word!

Proverbs 15:22–23

You have thrown the door to your dreams wide open. Now sit down with the people who know you best, and ask them what they see to be your strengths and weaknesses.

Seek counsel from your friends. They may be able to see things you can't because you are too close to your own situation to be objective. Try not to be defensive when receiving their advice, but listen with an open spirit.

Bring your ideas and the advice of your friends before the Lord and ask Him to help you sift through them.

Be aware, however, that there aren't many dreamers out there. Be careful with whom you share your heart's desires. You don't need a cold splash in the face just when you are getting the courage to jump in.

Dare to dream, seek godly human advice, and then bring it all to God so together you can throw out the rocks and polish the jewels of truth.

18

What's Most Important to You?

Lord, walking in the way of your laws, we wait for you; your name and renown are the desire of our hearts. My soul yearns for you in the night; in the morning my spirit longs for you.

Isaiah 26:8–9

What do you want most? Does your heart yearn for God in the night? Does your spirit long for Him in the morning? At night it often seems that all I yearn for is uninterrupted sleep, and in the morning, the first thing I think about is usually breakfast.

Only God can make the desire for Him first in our lives. Pray that He will fill you with longing for His presence. We are promised that our dream to be close to Him will come true.

19

THINK ON WHAT IS GOOD

Finally, brothers, whatever is true, whatever is noble, whatever is right, whatever is pure, whatever is lovely, whatever is admirable—if anything is excellent or praiseworthy—think about such things.

Philippians 4:8

What delights you? What are the things which give you pleasure? For the next few days notice your moments of joy and make a list of all the things that cause you gladness. Don't try to analyze what *should* bring you happiness. Instead, just notice what *does.*

There is so much good in every day. Often amidst the disappointments and hurt we miss the tiny joys that can help us persevere. For me, sometimes, it's as simple as how the dirt feels when I weed my pansies or the way the autumn sun stretches shadows across our backyard. It's the sweet hug my husband gives me for no special reason or my three-year-old's musical giggle.

Practice noticing the good that "just happens." Then begin to plan for good. Stuff as many of the things that delight you into your day as you can. Let the joy that comes from your delight spill over onto others as you think of ways to delight them. *Whatever is just, pure and good; think on these things.*

20

ACTION AND FAITH

Trust in the Lord and do good; dwell in the land and enjoy safe pasture. Delight yourself in the Lord and he will give you the desires of your heart. Commit your way to the Lord.

Psalm 37:3–5

Lord, you establish peace for us; all that we have accomplished you have done for us.

Isaiah 26:12

In Psalm 37:3–5 each verse begins with a verb—trust, delight, commit. We are called to participate in our relationship with God, and yet only He can give us the desire to do so. God wants us to dream, plan, and work, but all that we accomplish comes from Him.

21

THE WORKS PREPARED FOR YOU

For it is by grace you have been saved, through faith—and this not from yourselves, it is the gift of God—not by works, so that no one can boast. For we are God's workmanship, created in Christ Jesus to do good works, which God prepared in advance for us to do.

Ephesians 2:8–10

Nothing we do can save us. Our very best efforts are tainted with selfishness, yet we are created to do good works. God has prepared things for us to do. We are the most joyful and fulfilled when our heart's desires match up with that which God has prepared for us.

It's easy to be involved in several "good" things, and to not concentrate on God's "best." When I was in college I was so excited about serving the Lord that everything looked like an opportunity. I led a Bible study, was vice president of a campus ministry, and involved in a prison ministry.

I also was resident advisor, belonged to Baptist Student Union, worked with deaf children, helped the handicapped students, sang in the church choir . . . and occasionally studied. None of these things was bad, but because I was trying to do them all I wasn't able to do my best at any of them.

God began to teach me that no matter how good an opportunity to serve seems, if it isn't what He has called me to do, then I shouldn't pursue it.

Ask God to show you the works which He has prepared for you. Then pursue them wholeheartedly.

22

SEARCH YOUR HEART

The purposes of a man's heart are deep waters,
but a man of understanding draws them out.

Proverbs 20:5

As you look for new direction, you will find that you have to examine your heart. God knows our hearts completely, but like divers we must swim through deep waters to find the treasures hidden there.

For us, swimming around in our hearts is not natural or comfortable. Often we see dangerous and ugly things. More rarely, we find beautiful treasures, deposited there by God. But we have to search, bringing good and bad to the surface, then handing both to Him. He disposes of the ugly things, and then shows us the light of Christ reflected in the gleaming treasures.

23

BE CONFIDENT AND PERSEVERE

So do not throw away your confidence; it will be richly rewarded. You need to persevere so that when you have done the will of God, you will receive what he has promised.

Hebrews 10:35–36

God calls us to have confidence in Him and to persevere daily in our faith. When something doesn't come easy, it doesn't always mean that it isn't what God wants you to do. Oftentimes we reach our goals only after lengthy toil and effort.

Once you see the direction God wants you to go, persevere with confidence in Him.

24

BALANCE

He who works his land will have abundant food,
but he who chases fantasies lacks judgment.

Proverbs 12:11

In almost every area of our lives there is a need for balance. Sometimes, the things that are seen as contradictions in Scripture are really God's way of calling us to balance.

For instance, Ephesians 2:8–9 tells us that we have been saved by grace, not works. Then in James 2:17 we are told that faith is dead without deeds. These verses may seem to contradict one another, when actually they complement each other. In Ephesians, Paul did not say that works were not important; he said that works could not save us. And James did not teach that deeds would save us; he just wanted us to know that deeds are evidence of our faith.

Similarly, Proverbs 12:11 does not teach us not to dream; there are too many examples of godly dreamers in the Bible—Moses, Hannah, and Caleb are just a few. But this verse warns against chasing empty dreams.

As you seek to rebuild the dreams in your life, you must continually give them to God, asking for wisdom and judgment in your decisions. As you surrender your dreams to Him, He will give you the balance.

25

HANNAH'S DREAM

"I prayed for this child, and the Lord has granted
me what I asked of him. So now I give him to
the Lord. For his whole life he will be given over
to the Lord." And he worshiped the Lord there.

1 Samuel 1:28

Hannah had a dream. More than anything, she
wanted a son. She prayed and wept and her desire was
so consuming that she became physically ill from the
grief.

God answered Hannah's prayers and she was over-
joyed. Then she did something amazing. She gave her
answer to prayer—her heart's desire—right back to
God.

She didn't just release Samuel emotionally, but she
physically took him to the temple and left him there.
I can't imagine the courage that took.

Before my daughter Anna died, I was probably one
of the most careful moms you could have met. I was
extremely careful what I ate when I was pregnant and
very careful what my children ate when they grew
bigger. We always buckled seat belts and wore bicycle
helmets. And the kids were absolutely not allowed to
watch more than an hour and a half of supervised TV
a day. All this was done to help them grow up healthy
and strong.

Then Daniel was born with Down's syndrome and Anna died of cancer. I had done everything humanly possible to keep them healthy, but all my best efforts were for naught.

I'm not saying that parents shouldn't try their best to watch over their children. Of course they should. But the bottom line is that our children don't really belong to us. Everything we cherish belongs to God, and we have to be willing to surrender it all to Him.

26

CALEB'S FAITH

Then Caleb silenced the people before Moses and said, "We should go up and take possession of the land, for we can certainly do it."

Numbers 13:30

But because my servant Caleb has a different spirit and follows me wholeheartedly, I will bring him into the land he went to, and his descendants will inherit it.

Numbers 14:24

Caleb saw the same giants in Canaan the others saw. But he believed they could take the land because God was with them.

No obstacle is unconquerable when you are following God wholeheartedly. But I never feel sure I am wholehearted enough. I take many steps with far less confidence than Caleb. When obstacles loom, I wonder, *Is this really what God wants me to do?* Had I been in Caleb's shoes, I can hear myself saying, "Maybe these giants are God's way of closing the door."

It is often difficult to know what God wants. Some things in Scripture are clear and there is no doubt, but in other areas, God leaves room for His Spirit to lead each of us in different directions.

Part of faith is stepping out slowly, even when we don't feel secure in pursuit of our dreams, and then praying for Caleb's "different spirit" and the ability to follow God with our whole hearts.

27

IT'S NOT FAIR!

When morning came, there was Leah! So Jacob said to Laban, "What is this you have done to me? I served you for Rachel, didn't I? Why have you deceived me?" Laban replied, "It is not our custom here to give the younger daughter in marriage before the older one. Finish this daughter's bridal week; then we will give you the younger one also, in return for another seven years of work." And Jacob did so. He finished out the week with Leah, and then Laban gave him his daughter Rachel to be his wife.

Genesis 29:25–28

Jacob was in love with beautiful Rachel. She was his dream wife. He worked for her seven years. Laban deceived him and gave him Rachel's sister instead.

Jacob could have left Padden Aran a broken man. But his love for Rachel was great, so he promised to work for Laban another seven years. Finally, he and Rachel were married.

Sometimes our efforts are thwarted, not by our own sin but by the sin of others. We want to scream, "It's not fair!" and we are right—it isn't! Somehow we have to accept this reality without giving up. We must push ahead with a willingness to wait for the Lord.

28

WE'RE ALIENS

All these people were still living by faith when they died. They did not receive the things promised; they only saw them and welcomed them from a distance. And they admitted that they were aliens and strangers on earth.

Hebrews 11:13

Do you ever feel like an alien? Do you ever sit in a room full of people and think, *Are these folks wondering which flying saucer dropped me off?*

The truth is, we *don't* belong here. This is a foreign land, and we are on a long journey to get home. The paths available to us are choices we each must make.

We will find ourselves asking, *Do I pick the smooth, wide road, or the rocky, narrow one? Do I follow the paths lighted by Scripture, or do I forge ahead in the dark on my own?*

There will be consequences to my choices. Sometimes I will get lost. Sometimes the terrain will be so rough that I will get lost through no fault of my own. But, because I am God's child, I will complete the journey. I will make it home, and if I'll only reach for His hand, my Father will lead me there.

29

DAVID'S DREAM

After the king was settled in his palace and the Lord had given him rest from all his enemies around him, he said to Nathan the prophet, "Here I am, living in a palace of cedar, while the ark of God remains in a tent."

"'The Lord declares to you that the Lord himself will establish a house for you: When your days are over and you rest with your fathers, I will raise up your offspring to succeed you, who will come from your own body, and I will establish his kingdom. He is the one who will build a house for my Name, and I will establish the throne of his kingdom forever.'"

2 Samuel 7:1–2, 11–13

David had a dream. He wanted to build a "house" for God. It was a wonderful dream, but God had a different plan. David sought the counsel of Nathan, and through him God revealed that David's descendents would fulfill the dream. But in God's plan, the "house" would be a lineage and out of the lineage would come the Savior of the world.

When I was twenty-seven, I had the opportunity to spend a week with my natural father. It was the first time I had seen him in several years and probably only the fourth time since my parents' divorce when I was four. During that week I was able to share the gospel with him. Three months later he was diagnosed with terminal cancer. We corresponded over the next months, and when he no longer had the strength to read, I sent him Bible tapes to listen to. I believe he received Christ before his death.

His mother—my grandmother—was a Christian. I know from my conversations with him that she spent a lot of time in prayer for her son. She died when he was a very young man, but I believe her prayers reached across the generations to my heart and then to his. Though she didn't see it, her life made a difference.

As we reach for goals in this lifetime, we have to remember that what we do here doesn't always end when we are gone. Our lives have purpose in God's plan for the future, and some of our dreams may be fulfilled when we are not here to see them.

30

The Most Extraordinary Dream

However, as it is written: "No eye has seen, no
ear has heard, no mind has conceived what God
has prepared for those who love him."

1 Corinthians 2:9

Try, for a moment, to imagine your life filled with
every good thing, with every dream fulfilled. Now,
with that picture in mind, try to really understand
that what God has prepared for you in heaven is far
more wonderful than you are able to envision.

Heaven is the *most* marvelous hope, the *most* ex-
traordinary dream, and the God of the universe has
promised His children that *it will come true!*

31

My Prayer for You

May the God of hope fill you with all joy and peace
as you trust in him, so that you may overflow with
hope by the power of the Holy Spirit.

Romans 15:13

This verse is my prayer for you. My prayer for each of
you who have lost a dream is that you will find new
hope in God.

New hope doesn't take away the pain. Some losses will always sadden our hearts. But hope for the future gives us the strength to continue on, to run the race, to persevere. It gives us the ability to complete the journey even if we have to carry a load of pain to the end. Hope in God guarantees we will not have to carry the burden alone and that one day it will be lifted from us, forever.

EPILOGUE

THE BIRTH OF NEW DREAMS

During summers between college terms I worked at the elementary school in my hometown. One summer I became great friends with a girl I worked with named Beverly. We teased each other about being related since our surnames were the same but she was black and I was Caucasian.

One day she walked in looking sad. I asked her what was wrong and she said, "Robin, I'm just going through changes." I had never heard that expression before but have since come to appreciate it as an appropriate and vivid way to describe the ups and downs in our lives.

We all go through changes. I never ended up teaching deaf children as I had planned. With a handicapped child my family was very different from my earlier dreams. Being a mom was harder than I ever imagined. All of these things were changes and took some adjustment of expectations.

With some of the changes in our lives there is only a moment's hesitation, like hitting a pot hole in the road. With others it seems as if the road ends at a great chasm and there is no way to move on and get past the terrible emptiness. But God's grace is big enough to reach across even the deepest of pits, and in two ways He began to reach over and help me rebuild a bridge of dreams.

First, about two years after Anna died, as I drove home from Daniel's physical therapy, I began to pray. We had applied for adoption and had been waiting over a year. That is a short time as far as adoptions go, but Caleb was already ten and we really hoped our baby would come before he grew too much older. I asked God to please send our baby daughter soon. In my heart I heard Him say, "I'll send your baby after you write this book for Me."

I had been thinking about writing a devotional for people who are grieving. While I was in the middle of all my hurt, I marked all the verses in my Bible that brought me comfort—and they weren't the usual verses that people quote in difficult times. I thought these different verses might help someone else, but I hadn't yet started writing. As soon as I got home that day I began. I wrote for three days straight, and then spent a couple of weeks reviewing and adding to it. Our daughter, Lydia Grace, was born about the time I finished the book, though she didn't come to live with us until a month later.

Several months after that, I had lunch with our pastor's wife and told her about the book. She read it and encouraged me to send it out. That was the beginning of my writing.

I worked out one and sometimes two days a week with a babysitter, and I went to the library to write. I started to crave the time I could spend writing. Before long I realized that being a writer had been a dream of mine for many years. Somehow, along the way it had been forgotten.

One day our son Caleb wanted to look through my scrapbooks to see what I was like when I was his age. I found my first rejection letter; when I was nine years old I had sent a poem to *Reader's Digest.* I also found a seventh grade newspaper with several articles that I had written and a high school magazine that had published a couple of my poems.

In all the busyness of being a wife and mother and then in all the pain, I had lost who I was. I had completely forgotten my dream of writing children's books. I had forgotten that I liked unusual clothes and bright colors, and I had forgotten what a crazy sense of humor I had. Slowly, God brought all of these things back into my life and with my personal growth came healing.

The second thing that happened was that I began to really appreciate the special family God had given me. Each of my precious children has very special needs, and there are days when their needs overwhelm me. But along with their specialness comes unspeakable joy.

Our son Caleb took the SAT in the seventh grade for the Talent Identification Program at Duke University. His scores were very high, and we were invited to Duke for a special weekend recognition ceremony and conference. At the conference the speakers talked about the special needs of gifted children and how as parents we have to make sure they have enough challenges to be happy.

Instead of my challenging Caleb, he has always challenged me. He accepted Christ at a young age and has challenged me with questions like, "If God is love, then does that mean He loves Satan?"

Living with Daniel is like living with an angel. I know it is theologically impossible, but I have never seen any sin in his little life. He just wants to love and be loved. There is a sweetness in him that is unexplainable.

When Lydia was two and a half she was diagnosed with ADHD (Attention Deficit and Hyperactivity Disorder). In Lydia's busyness there is an enthusiasm for life that is contagious. To walk to our house from the car we have to pass a rose bush. Lydia *always* stops to smell the fragrant pink blossoms, and she won't let me go in until I smell them too. She delights in a bubble bath and refuses to get out till every bubble is gone. She adores eating spaghetti and experiences it so thoroughly that it takes me an hour to get all the sticky noodles off her and the surrounding furniture. With Lydia around I won't miss anything. She makes sure I pay attention to the everyday joys.

I pray that if you are feeling trapped and hopeless in the loss of your dreams, God will somehow use this devotional to light the tiny spark of hope that will get you going. No matter how trapped we feel, God always leaves a way out. Sometimes you can find that way by beginning to make very small changes in your life.

My life is very different from what I dreamed about. But it is what God has chosen for me. It is God's dream for me, and His dream is much better than I could ever have imagined.